Daddy Tell Me About The Rastaman

by
John M. Moodie

authorHOUSE®

AuthorHouse™
1663 Liberty Drive
Bloomington, IN 47403
www.authorhouse.com
Phone: 833-262-8899

Published by AuthorHouse 09/23/2020

ISBN: 978-1-4259-4999-0 (sc)
ISBN: 978-0-7596-0327-1 (e)

Print information available on the last page.

Any people depicted in stock imagery provided by Getty Images are models, and such images are being used for illustrative purposes only. Certain stock imagery © Getty Images.

This book is printed on acid-free paper.

Dedicated to I n I two daughters Monica and Kiesha.
And to all children of JAH.

SELAH SEE I

It was a late spring morning, I sat under the mango tree deep into thought, I did not realize that Tamika had snuck up behind me. "Boo" she said, her smile reflects the beauty of the spring morning.

"Daddy what are you doing?" "Oh, just meditating" I replied. "About what, your God?" "Yes Tamika and the beautiful morning." We sat in slience for a few seconds. I knew there is something she want to ask me.

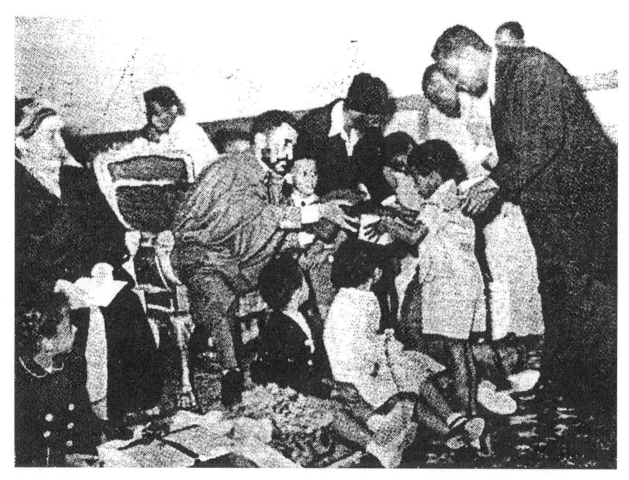

The Emperor presenting Christmas gifts to children at an orphanage.

"What's' on your mind sweetheart?" I asked her. She turn her gaze at me and with those innocent brown eyes she said, "Daddy tell me about the Rastaman." I smiled, said a silent prayer and began.

One day long time ago in the Island of Jamaica, around the early 1920's. There was this man name Marcus Mosiah Garvey. The Rastafarians see him as a prophet. He would go around preaching and teaching the people to be concious of themselves. He taught them to be proud of their African heritage.

Marcus Garvey's aim was to take black people back to Africa and rebuild the continent. His organization was called the U.N.I.A. United Negro Improvement Association. One day while preaching to his followers, He told them to look to Africa where a black king would be crowned, for the day of Africa's redemption is at hand.

The people heard him but did not take him seriously. Then on November 2nd 1930, in the land of Euthiopia a prince by the name of Ras Tafari Makonnen was crowned King of Kings and lord of lords, conquering lion of the tribe of Judah, light of the world, and root of David.

"Do you understand what I just said?" "Yes daddy, so his name was Ras Tafari. I *see*" she said, "so that's why they call you Rastafari?" "Yes sweetheart, the *bible* told us that the children of Jah shall be called by his name." She looked puzzled. "Whats wrong?" I said to her, "I am just wondering how come his name is Haile Selassie and his name is Rastafari?"

"You see Tamika when he was born he was baptized 40 days after his birth. At his baptism the bishop gave him his true name Haile Selassie I. This name means Power of the Trinity. When he became King, he took on his baptismal name Haile Selassie the first since he was the first one to have that name."

Haile Selassie I (Last of the Solomonic Kings) H.I.M. Negusa Negast, His Imperial Majesty Haile Selassie I (Power of the Holy Trinity) Emperor of Ethiopia, King of Kings, Lord of Lords, Conquering Lion of the Trib e of Judah, Elect of God, Light of the Universe – displaying here the mystical and metaphysical "Salutation of Peace" or the sign of the Hily Trinity. The triangle pointing downwards is an esoteric symbol representing the material phase of the Seal ot Solomon; the six pointed star is also known as the Star of David.

"you said his name means Power of the Trinity, what is Trinity? daddy."

"Trinity means three in one. Jah the father, Jah the son, and Jah the Highest spirit. Take dad for example, I am a father, I am a son, and I have the Highest spirit in me. Yet I am one person. So Haile Selassie being the Power of the Trinity has the power over all Trinities."

"I understand daddy, tell me more it is very interesting." After Haile Selassie was crowned many people in Jamaica began to remember what Marcus had said and began to search the bible to see if this man could be the return messiah. Jah in person. They know Jesus must return to earth to claim his glory and collect his children. So they were looking for him."

"There was a few preachers who were followers of Garvey, Lenoard Howell, Joseph Hibbert, Bedward and Archibald Dunkley. These men made an in-depth search of the bible and were convinced that Haile Selassie was Jesus of Nazareth return to earth. They began to preach this message to the people."

Bro. Josiah Hibbert in ceremonial Regalia.

"Daddy are you telling me that there are places in the bible that show these people and you too daddy that this man is God or Jah as you call him." Lets see if we can walk the path Howell, Bedward, Hibbert and Dunkley took. Lets get the bible and try to see this for ourselves," I said.

Tamika ran inside to get the bible while I asked the father for wisdom to teach my daughter the truth as I see it. When she return I open the bible to Genesis 49 verse 10. "You see Tamika, Haile Selassie is from the line of Judah and according to this verse, it will be Judah that all nations will bow down and praise, it will be Judah that will have the scepter and it will be through Judah that Shiloh will return."

Haile Selassie, the Ethiopian King, Mounted on a White Horse. That Pawed in the Valley of Armageddon, and Disturbed the Waters of the Seven Seas from Gibraltar to Mandalay

"Who is Shiloh and what is a scepter daddy?" Shiloh is the creator of the universe and a scepter is a rod of dominion given to a King. "So you mean Haile Selassie is Shiloh?" "Yes Tamika and as the bible tells you that unto him shall the gathering of the people be. So it is him that the Rastafarians are gathering to bow down and praise."

"So why do you wear your hair like that and uncle "D" is a Rasta and he don't wear locks." "I took a oath unto father that I will wear my hair like this until a time that I have specified. Lets turn the bible to Numbers chapter 6. It tells of the nazerite vow, which all Rastafarians who wear there hair in locks took. Jesus was a nazerite, he took the same oath. If you can picture Jesus as a Black man you would see him looking like a dreadlocks man."

"Tell me more daddy." In Psalms 132 Jah promised David that of the fruit of his loins he would sit on David throne. This means that from the family tree of David, Jah himself would come on earth and sit on David's throne. David's throne is in Ethiopia and that's the same throne that Haile Selassie I sat upon. It could not have been Jesus because he did not sit upon a throne when he first came on earth. He must return to fulfil this prophecy."

H.I.M the Emperor, eleven years old, with his father, Ras Makonnen

"Now let's turn to Isaiah chapter 9, which tells us that a child would be born whose name shall be called wonderful, counselor, the everlasting father, the almighty God. This son according to Isaiah, would sit on David's throne and bring his kingdom to order. Haile Selassie has fulfil all of these prophasies. Again Tamika, after Jesus left the earth he promised to return. In this coming, he would not be a lamb to be killed. He would be the conquering lion."

"He would not return a peasant for them to spit on him and jeer him, putting a crown of thorns on his head. This time he would come as King of Kings and Lord of Lords with a crown of gold, for the world to praise and glorify him. In Acts chapter 2, Peter one of Jesus's disciples, told some people that God had sworn unto David that he would raise up Jesus to sit on David's throne. "Daddy this is a lot, Is Rasta a religion?"

"Over the years since Howell, Bedward, Dunkley and Hibbert Rasta has been upgraded by society from a cult to a valid religion. However Rasta see themselves as a Truth that must reach the four corners of the earth. Our truth is simple but people seem to find it hard to accept." What is that truth daddy?" "Our truth is that Haile Selassie is Jah almighty, Jesus in his Kingly character."

"Daddy are there more places in the bible that points to Haile Selassie as God.?" "Oh yes baby, when Archibald Dunkley, Bedward, Joseph Hibbert and Lenoard Howell read Revelation chapter 5, they saw that there was a book sealed with seven seals that no one could open. The prophet John wept, because there was no one on the earth or under the earth who was worthy to open this book or even to look upon it."

BEHOLD THE LAMB
And round avout the throne, were four beasts full of eyes before and behind.
The first beast was like a lion, and the second beast was like a calf,
and the third beast had a face like a man, and the fourth beast was like a flying eagle.
And the four and twenty elders fell down before him that sat upon the throne.

"And an angel said to John weep not, because the lion of Judah root and offspring of David has prevailed to open the book and look into it." "When Mosely and Dunkley saw this they were joyful because Haile Selassie is the Lion of Judah so it must be him who was worthy to open the seals of this book. Then they saw in Revelation 19 that his name was King of Kings and lord of lords. Knowing this truth they began to spread there truth and so Rastafari was born."

"When this truth that Rasta came forth with began to take hold, the people and government of Jamaica began trying to destroy it. The Rastaman was called crazy, he was put in jail, the police harassed them and cut their locks sometimes with machete and knives. Even the families of Rastafarians began to treat them bad. Mothers and Fathers disowned their children because they were calling on their God."

"That's terrible daddy," "Yes sweetheart but that's the way it was. And these Rasta knew that this would happen to them because God told them in the bible that their mother and their father would forsake them for his name sake. So Rasta developed a faith from inside. "You see Tamika, Rasta is taught from inside. It is what we refer to as an inborn concept. That's why your uncle is a Rasta and he does not wear locks. He worships Haile Selassie as his God and that's who he prays and give praises to but he does not have the locks. Still he is a Rasta. Therefore anytime a person finds himself and praise Haile Selassie I as their Jah and Saviour they become a child of Father and he is now a Rasta."

In a meeting with Pope Paul VI at the Vatican

"So daddy, to be a Rasta is to praise and worship Haile Selassie as God."

"Yes baby, that's Rasta. You take on his name."

"There is a spirit that dwells within all of us, once you find the creator, that spirit comes alive and begans to teach you all you need to know about Jah and his universe. This spirit you heard them refer to in church as the comforter. It is this spirit that we know as the spirit of Selassie. The highest spirit. Power of the Trinity." "So daddy is Rasta and Christianity the same? They both talk about Jesus."

Haile Selassie in palace courtyard, being presented a flower basket by the Patriarch of the Ethiopian Church at the Feast of the Finding of the True Cross.

"For anyone to be a Rasta, he must first accept Jesus. As a Rastaman we see him as a black man with dreadlocks. In this acceptance we become Christians. However we move further from Christianity and identify Haile Selassie as Jesus in his second coming. Christians are still waiting for Jesus to return while Rasta say he has already come in the personage of Haile Selassie who proclaims to be the light of the world. The tittles that Haile Selassie proclaims are the same tittles that Jesus must return with."

"The difference between Christianity and Rasta is that, Christianity says they are waiting for him to return, when Rasta said he has already come." "Like a thief in the night, right daddy?" "You are so smart Tamika, yes like a thief in the night." "One last question daddy and this is a tough one, If Haile Selassie is God how come he is dead?"

"It is not a tough question Tamika it is one I get asked all the time. Remember I told you that Jah was father, Jah was the son and that Jah was the highest spirit?" "Yes daddy, the trinity." "Right, well it was Jah the father who took Moses and the children of Israel out of Egypt, whom by the way are our forefathers. It was Jah the son who came as Jesus and conquered death and it will be Jah the spirit that will judge the world. So for Jah the father and Jah the son so we can see him in flesh to know him before he moves on to the spiritual form."

"Remember, I told you he is Jah the son who conquered death therefore death has no power over him. Jesus said we must worship him in spirit and in truth. When Rasta worship Jah in spirit, they can see jah as a father, because he is a father, They can see him as Jah Rastafari the son and they can picture him in their spiritual mind as Jah their King sitting on his throne with Empress Menen. And the truth about all this is they know who he is and what he looks like, they have a image of their God in their spiritual mind."

"So Jah is in spirit and it is up to his children, the Rastafarians, to take this truth to the four corners of the world. They will show the world that the return messiah has come and shined his light upon the world because he is the light of the world, earths rightful ruler. It is up to us to tell the world that Jesus has returned like a thief in the night while they were sleeping and did not see when he came. "He left his mark on the world as the greatest leader to walk the earth with such glory and majesty."

"Thanks daddy, you know so much about the Rastaman, I really enjoy talking to you." Tamika ran inside taking the bible with her. I smiled as she left, thanked the Father and listened to the nightingale as she sang her message to those who have ears to hear her."

The Unfolding Universe

In the beginning there was no word,
There was an experience before the word.
It was Jah who had a thought,
And from that thought came the word.

Jah for sure experience the world ,
Knowing that his experience and word must pass through.
Many came and carry their share,
Yet they all fall short of reaching home.

Jesus of Nazareth was the strongest of them all;
He took it through death and did not fall.
A lighted path he left for I n I,
To take with us home an experience and a word.

To the place it first began,
Africa seat of the rising sun.
Where the Lion of Juda
Root of David still prevail.

With Love I Cling

Great master and holy one of Rastafari,
I give thanks for the life I hold.
Thou oh master, is the invisible light
Of truth and righteousness.
The righteous judge of creation.
Unto thee, does the birds look to for food,
The lion for shelter and I for life.,
You dear father is the Jah of my fathers,
Be my guide in these days I need you,
Turn not from I oh Jah;
Redeem I from thy wrath
And let I give praises to thy name.
Let me tell the world of how just is I Jah.
Open my eyes oh Jah and let thy light shine in;
Cover me with thy great arm
For my enemies are at my heel;
They wait for your sheep like a starving wolf;
You dear Jah will not let I fall;
But will guide I through the narrow path to life.
Blessed hath thou, oh Jah Rastafari;
You are a righteous father and I love you.

John Moodie

Stolen

My root, my root where are you?
Stolen from me and now I am lost;
Lost in the abyss of Babylon,
Stumbling to find an identity and a way.

My history! My history they stole you too?
Destitute I am to shame and poverty,
Stumbling through this darken maze
Looking for light where there is no day.

Mockingly they taught me to pray;
Looking into the sky for a great white god,
That would come one day,
And feed I with milk and honey so they say.

They tell me I am from Africa,
Where the jungle and people so uncivilized.
The great white Tarzan they proudly say;
Will bring this continent from its darken way.

My history! My root! I hear you cry,
Deep in my heart I hear you sigh;
Look for yourself, for they tell you a lie;
My history my root you look so old and abused;
Yet you are still a jewel for I.

The Legendary Cross

To the four corners of the world, mankind was dispersed,
    What a confusion;
Upon the cross was Jesus crucified,
    What a cover up;
Upon the light post is the cross,
    What a shock;
Here I am at the cross roads,
    What a accident;
Upon the grave is the cross,
    What a mourning;
In the church the cross is raised high,
    What a praising;
Boy you are full of crosses,
    What a state of emergency.

John Moodie

Rasta Jah Messengers

Sing your messages oh messengers of Jah
Jah Jah train is now on the move;
Sound the trumpets of redemption
And let the sheep hear the Shepherd's call.

Let your light shine bright oh knotty Dread;
For Rastafari is Jah light of this world.
Sing songs for his Almighty Jah
For he has come the Conquering Lion.

Messengers of Jah, let your light shine,
Jah has placed you above the stars of Babylon,
So chant your messages and chant them loud
For you're the sheep of Jah's pasture.

Let your light shine bright Niyaman
It will burn those who try to put it out;
Hold that light high oh mighty Rastafari
For you are Jah chosen warriors.

John Moodie

Look Within

As I search for Jah one day,
I saw two birds at play.
How do I find my creator I say?
They stop, look at me and say,
Twit Twit!! Twit Twit!!
And they both flew away.
Twit Twit I say
As I continue on my way,
Twit Twit and I began to pray.
Then softly I hear a voice say,
Twit Twit, I am here always
Never too far I am here to stay.
And so, on that day
Just as the birds say;
Look within!! Look within!!
I found Jah as I pray.

John Moodie

The Taste of True Life

Sweeter is true life than all the spices
Of Kedar and the African coast;
Sweeter than the life of this world;
Men search high and low for a taste,
Only to find the sting of death awaits.
Put all the gold of Africa of old
And all the diamonds and pearls of her womb;
Let them dazzle in the mid-day sun,
Their beauty is only a gravel of sand
Compare to true life.
Its beauty is Rastafari,
Light of this world.
Taste of this tree oh holy children,
It is music to thy belly
And food for thy eyes;
It is sweeter than a crying baby's tears,
For you have no tears to cry,
It's sweetness is compass
Only by the taste of true life,
For true life, is the sweetness of freedom.

John Moodie

Africa Arise

Cry! Cry! Oh children of Africa,
Let your tears flood the river Nile,
Let your mourns be heard by the wind;
And let Africa arise.

For too long, oh mother land,
You have allowed us to roam wild;
Too long, we've slave for the world,
Its time, oh mother take us home.

We are despised by the world,
From the blue eyed, to the cross eyed.
They treat us as dirt of the world;
How long oh mother land, how long?

We 've been stripped of our dignity,
Our history and our pride;
What more will you let them take?
Oh mother land, not out King.

Arise!! Africa!! Arise,
And let the fragrance of your bosom
Revive the youth of your blood,
And the food of your stomach strengthen them.

Arise oh mother and show the world
Who is the Conquering Lion;
For thou the elephant is big and strong
Its the cunningness and speed of the lion
That makes him master,
So arise!! my blessed mother land, Africa Arise.

John Moodie

Jah Live

I know Selassie live
I know Rastafari live
I know the Lion reign
In the heart of I n I

He took away I burden
And lay them on his shoulder
He took away my troubles
And lay them straight before me

He took away my sins
And nail them on the cross
He took away my fear
And show I who he is

He came no more a lamb
But as a Lion of Judah
He came no more a peasant
But as the King of Kings

The seven seals he has broken
The book of life are now open
Trumpets are now sounding
Righteous ones he is calling

I know Selassie I live
I know Rastafari live

John Moodie

History Beyond History

The hieroglyphics on the base of my father's pyramid,
The Negroid features, on the base of the Sphinx of the Delta Nile;
Tells me, I have a history beyond history.
When the archeologist points his torch,
Where history were written on books of stone,
I see the fingers and faces of my fathers;
I rejoice, for I have a history beyond history.
As the Mathematician solve his equations;
The Scientist puts his rockets in space;
Even as the Architect puts up his high rise buildings,
I see the hands of my fathers,
Yes I have a history beyond history.
Everyday more discoveries in my fathers homeland;
Of millions of years that they were here,
Shining their light even to this day.
I sometimes smile to know that I know,
That I have a history beyond history.

John Moodie

The Chariot Is Ready

Upon the rock of the air I build I chariot
A rock the evil cannot see
Yet the inner soul of I hold firm
Upon the rock of His Almighty Jah

When I walk, I walk inside my chariot
When I sleep, the walls of I chariot covers I
The invisible wall I only feel
The rock is Almighty Jah

Water nor fire penetrates not I rock
Truth and righteousness are tickets for a ride
Hop on oh holy children of Jah
This chariot is Zion bound

The Red Sea was no match for I rock
Neither will nuclear bomb or laser beam
What force can stop this chariot
For even death is dead

Jesus walk so Rasta could come forward
And conquer the darkness around his children's eyes
Open your eyes oh holy children
Rastafari has come to take you home

To the land of our fathers
The land of Holy Mount Zion
Hold firm on this invisible chariot
Moving through with its mystic vibration

Do not be frightened of the horns
They are only the cry of the Warriors
The dead will arise at such a cry
Even the trees will sing and dance
So hold firm Rasta Children
Jah Jah is the driver of this Zion bound chariot.

John Moodie

Red Gold And Green

Marvel not upon the colors of I crown,
It reveals more than the naked eyes behold.
More than a weak heart can withstand,
Upon it rules the Conquering Lion.

As a child of the sun, I remind the world of the rainbow;
As a child of Africa, the Liberation flag I hold.
As a child of Jah, I represent the signal light of life,
And not that of your cross roads.

Into this world I and I came,
A world of darkness hate and pain.
Blinded with lust and greed,
When Jah caution I, about the fire that burn red.

The inner I seeks the golden rough road;
Rocky it is but firmly and boldly I hold.
For truth and righteousness lights this way,
Where prayers are the food for the day.

For many are called , but only a few chose to come home
To see the green light that have been proven
Worthy, to bear the name of Rastafari;
And received the gift of everlasting life.

Red gold and green the colors of I crown;
Magnificently I wore the colors I adorn.
Liberation, Truth and Light,
Shines brightly, on this path for I.

A warrior Called

Oh mighty warrior of Jah,
You are summoned to be a Rastafari.
You have found favor in Jah sight,
And is called to be a warrior.
Let the words of your mouth,
The meditation of your heart;
Be accepted in Jah sight.
Armor your self with
Righteousness and truth.
The work of your hands,
Let it be your shield, righteousness.
For your sword, the words of your mouth, truth.
Plunge for the heart oh mighty warrior;
If he stands he will shield you.
Remember oh warrior of truth,
The elements of the universe are on your side;
They will rise up to defend you,
Only ask and they will obey;
The time has come when truth and right must win;
Cut them down with the bullet of truth;
And trod them down with righteousness.

John Moodie

Secret Agent of Jah Jah

Traveling down the road one day
Preaching and chanting Rastafari way
Giving praises and thanks to the most high.
As I chant the scriptures to a brother about Fari
A dreadlock sister was standing near
Utter a sound loud and clear
"Have you ever seen a Lion without his mane?"
Took a stock, the daughter was referring to I claim
To be a Rastafari without a crown
Was a mockery she chant a sound
I felt the spirit of Rastafari within I move strong
I turn to her and I chant a song
I am a bald head Rastafari
Secret agent of Selassie I
Carrying out the orders of Jah Jah plan
On a mission just like the dreadlocks man
Thou I may look like a lamb
I have the heart of a Conquering Lion
Judge I not from a distant
Test I heart for its content
Yes I am a bald head Rastaman
Secret agent of a higher plan
I am a bald head Rastafari
On a mission for Selassie I

I Call Him Jah Rastafari

Some call him the Rose of Sharon;
Some call him the Lilies of the Valley;
Some call him Jesus of Nazareth,
But I call him Jah Rastafari.

They call him the Prince of Peace;
They call him the Wonderful Councillor;
They call him the Almighty God;
But I call him Jah Rastafari.

He is the Lion of Judah;
He is the Root of David;
John spoke about him,
Opening the Book of the Seven Seals.

They proclaim him the King of Kings;
They proclaim him the Lord of Lords;
Peter spoke of him, reigning on David's Throne.
 Power of theTrinity is his name,
But unto I he is Jah Rastafari.

I call him Jah Rastafari;
I know he is the savior,
Jesus in his Kingly character;
But to I he is Jah Rastafari.

John Moodie

About the Author

This is the author's third book concerning the Truth about Rasta. John Moodie (or Ras Mikael as he is known to Rastafarians) is a very knowledgeable Rasta. He is not afraid to speak the Truth.

He is sure Haile Selassie I is Jesus of Nazareth returned in His kingly and conquering form. Born in Jamaica, Ras Mikael found Jah over twenty-four years ago and is very firm in his faith.

Printed in the United States
By Bookmasters